TEA WITH MARCEL PROUST

WORDS BY JUDY KRAVIS

PICTURES BY PETER MORGAN

ROAD BOOKS

Published in a limited edition of
900 copies, numbered 1 to 900.

433

Road Books
Garravagh
Inniscarra
County Cork
Ireland
1993.

British Library Cataloguing in Publication Data.
A catalogue record for this book is available
from the British Library.

ISBN 0 9519358 1 X

This book was sponsored by
UNIVERSITY COLLEGE CORK,
LE SERVICE CULTUREL DE L'AMBASSADE DE FRANCE À DUBLIN,
RHONE-POULENC RORER (NENAGH),
MINITEL (DUBLIN),
CHURCH AND GENERAL INSURANCE (DUBLIN).

Typesetting by Upper Case Ltd, Cork, Ireland
Printing by City Printing Works, Cork, Ireland

CONTENTS

INTRODUCTION

I've always liked the community of readers in *Fahrenheit 451* who learn their books by heart, become their books, walk them to and fro, adopt their names. I like readers who read outdoors. Alice's sister falls asleep reading on the river bank, then Alice sees the white rabbit. I like oblivious readers. My aunt Lily one Christmas reads *Alice in Wonderland* upside down while listening to Schubert's *Trout* quintet playing at the wrong speed. I like Borges' Pierre Menard who is such a good reader of *Don Quixote* that he manages to write it again word for word. Equally I like Jo in *Little Women* who reads in the attic and eats apples.

Tea With Marcel Proust is a promotion of language, a bazaar of reading, a reading life in french literature. You can read a poem and weigh it enough to translate it. You can read a chronology and know a life. You can scan a book you've read before and remember the gist, remember the person you were when you read it before, the feelings it provoked, the *correspondances* with who you were then, who you still are. You can read the title, read a sentence, feel the japanese flowers unfold out of Marcel Proust's cup of tea - you can make a picture.

The reader who takes liberties is a reader who does justice to the writer. If to write is to express freely, then to read freely is to pay tribute. I wrote these pieces to do justice and to pay tribute to writers with whom as reader and as teacher I have had a long relationship. I've made free with their works as their works made free with me. I've translated, conflated, imagined, impersonated; I've looked for and exploited connections with my own life. Honest reading is always like that.

In my dual language edition of Proust's essay *On Reading*, the translators, Autret and Burford, say they weren't seeking to turn Proust into a contemporary english or american writer. In my translations, stories, conversions of Proust, Baudelaire, Rimbaud, Alain-Fournier, Madame de Sévigné and Mallarmé, I've sought to do just that. I don't inhabit the same world as these 17th, 19th and early 20th century writers, and yet I do, I inhabit their words. I know these people like the back of my hand, like my pocket, I recognize their world in the one I live in. I haven't met them but I'd know them if I did.

Proust in 1993 wouldn't find a publisher. He'd be writing away, the manuscript in shoe boxes, in circumstances more reduced than he'd admit, in Neuilly. Baudelaire would be a singer-songwriter like Leonard Cohen, going from melancholia to cynicism in one mid-life swoop. Rimbaud would make music videos, then go into post-punk pre-dada film. Alain-Fournier would go to a therapist, become a pacifist and a teacher. Madame de Sévigné could translate across three centuries like Virginia Woolf's Orlando, into a series of strong and private women of whom the most recent might be Hélène Cixous, Germaine Greer or Marguerite Duras. As for Mallarmé, circa 1970 I was Mallarmé, several inches off the ground near Lewes, Sussex. I have inside information.

Judy Kravis 1993

FRENCH WITHOUT TEARS

I saw the ad in the paper while I was having my Saturday coffee and cheese bap up at Volta's: *Learn to Speak like a Native!* My friends have always said I was something of a natural for things I put my mind to, quick at picking up the new dances etcetera, and there's something about idleness in a steamy café on a Saturday that leads you into a bit of a dream. If you can speak like a native, where does that leave you and is it very different from this?

I didn't buy their line about enhancing your chances in today's world, but I like cutting round the scissor marks in the paper, so I sent off the form. It was strange how immediately I started to register this creeping frenchness there already was, from blue Nuits de Paris perfume bottles in Woolworths, to triumphant songs on the radio about regret or not. This in fact was Lesson One: the french you already know.

Lesson Two was the french you'd forgotten was french, like leeks au gratin and the pliés you did at ballet classes when you were six. I began to realise that being a native was quite radical and fine; tiny rootlets extended in every direction, invisible until translated though you must be growing them all the time. That was Lesson Three. It filtered through on the bus to and from work, which can get very introspective and reflective, especially winter nights.

Down on the salt marshes one Sunday I saw that strange plant on the mud at low tide, and remembered how someone had said the French would mortgage their grannies for a taste of it. It looked like tiny green skittles. I took some home and cooked it: it tasted like the air on the salt marshes in winter, thin and green. Lesson Four.

Nothing arrived in the post, but in the weeks that followed I learned fast. I saw a french singer on tv: Juliette Gréco was Lesson Five. Being native in french meant being a cat with half-closed eyes, if you were a woman. It meant clearing the space in front of you in the smoky jazz cellar (in the sky). Slinky, we used to call it at school. Or Chic. We defied each other: *you* could never be Chic. It lay beyond irregular verbs, beyond the pitiful world of Toto and Babette in our school textbook. Lesson Six was the realisation that all the french I learned at school would fit into a small chocolate cup cake.

Lesson Seven was a film about a pillow fight on tv. Subtitled. It was hard to read the subtitles and take in the story; or maybe it was less of a story and more of a dream about wise and canny french children, which all natives were once. How sophisticated a pillow fight could be, how meaningful and, dare I say it, how beautiful.

Lesson Eight was about beauty of another kind. I came across a copy of Paris-Match at the hairdresser's. Vanda, my regular, told me it was left by the french wife of that artist fella John who lived down by Osborne's bus station, Françoise, she was called. Vanda is always excellent on detail. She said I could have the magazine since it seemed I'd acquired this interest in things french, so I took it home and learned about the french Look and how it was already regarded as such in at least seventeen different countries, most of all in England and America. The cat woman was part of the Look, as well as a more pixie schoolgirl learning ambiguous lessons: the wise and canny child grows up. Swirls of cigarette smoke and a few very painted-looking swooshing side waves of black hair made the Look into a seascape on a Spring day. My hair only swooshes when it's wet. And far from poised in flattering breezes, up here on the East Coast I'm more likely to be struggling in the teeth of a gale with a button off my mac.

Lesson Nine was a show-stopper. I was actually in mid-flight down the High Street having left home without my purse and had to tear back in order to get the bus. It was in the record shop window: Lesson Nine. Printed on a card with a hand pointing.

Stop Right Here. Turn around slowly. Draw a circle three metres wide. Inside that circle there are many thousands of unseen french things. Find some of them.

I stepped outside my circle only momentarily to put a call through to the boss and tell him I wouldn't be in today, my back was that bad again; and then again just for a quick coffee and bap up at Volta's because I'm sure any native would agree you can't discover much on an empty stomach. Then I went back to the record shop, read the instructions again, and a few record covers, then for the nth time the notice they always have on their door about Everything For The Beekeeper Except Bees. Puzzling, the record shop, therefore very native and french you could say, and all without a french record in sight. Unless: *I Can Hear The Whistle Blow* by Richard Anthony. He looked french enough to score several points. I went into the shop and asked if they would put it on for me. Amazing how the place was transformed into a bit of *parlez-vous*, all the schoolgirl french flooding the cracks.

Lesson Ten did come through the post, which was a relief. You wouldn't like to think you were making it all up. I played Richard Anthony as I read it through. When I say read, I mean, passed my eyes across. It was all in french and my lessons to that point hadn't prepared me for the actual language. So I kept Lesson Ten by and toyed with it sometimes over breakfast to see if any more words had shone through, which some did, surprisingly; they began to look familiar, like the back of the cornflakes packet which I always read until it goes strange and I can't understand a word, even less than french. Breakfast is a quietly testing time, especially if you live on your own.

Unfortunately I hadn't kept the original ad which had told me how many lessons to expect, and I wasn't sure whether or not I was native yet, to say nothing of enhanced, but I was keeping my eyes peeled. And my ears. And I'd nosed out just about everything french in our town, short of calling on the artist's french wife. She must be Lesson Eleven.

From then on I gave up going to Volta's on a Saturday morning. I went down to Françoise instead. A couple of years of Saturday mornings, it turned out to be, and a good few evenings as well. I soon felt I could listen to her for ever. I loved the way her face went as she talked, the way she held her cup and slung her opinions across the room. It was a very small room; the rough walls were painted lavender with opinions all over them. I went round for dinner quite often. Françoise made salads about six feet across and couscous that brought home the true meaning of eating too much: a sort of expanding granary around the entire midriff region. Not that Françoise was fat, no, she had the oho-I-know pixie look I'd registered in her magazines, but she had a regard for food the way the English have a regard for christenings or dogs.

It turned out that the inscrutable Lesson Ten I'd received in the post was a recipe, at least it was in the style of a recipe, since it didn't sound like anything you could actually make, not without a lifetime and a full set of encyclopaedias, but Françoise got a laugh out of it and John even more. The time I took it round we were having John's Special Pancakes, which had taken him all afternoon. It was his only dish so it had to be Special, he explained. But it was a blink in the divine eye of Lesson Ten which began: *Il faut cultiver ses artichauts.* First grow your artichokes.

Françoise would often drop a few words of french into her talk, more as time went by, so I started to absorb this groundswell of things she found untranslatable, the exclamations, frustrations, the boredom phrases and the pissed-off words. She started lending me books too, some in french and english on opposite pages; these I read across, to and fro, making a ghostly third page in between. For the first time since we had to learn *Meg Merilees* by heart at school when I was about 9, I read poetry. I started to enjoy floating about between stanzas, among words I couldn't always understand: chunks of words, chunks of time.

I can't tell you what this multiplication of my inner life did to my relations with my boss. Suffice to say he was curious, but I told him nothing. This sort of *hauteur,* Françoise assured me, was very french and probably Lesson Twelve. So far so good. My chances were definitely enhanced now I knew how to keep silent. "Did you ever think of going to France?" John asked and I laughed. I hadn't been further than Frinton-on-sea and wasn't planning to. Besides, the course was far too good. Lessons could be infinite.

My friends were saying they hardly saw me any more. I was always home with my head in a french book and my feet in a french record. Re-living Françoise's childhood, would be another way of putting it. All the books she'd ever had since she started reading, she said. There weren't many but they were of a kind: about children who inhabited separate worlds and lost them or found them or drowned in them. I was never sure whether it was the mysteriousness of the books meeting the mysteriousness of the french in my head or a taste I'd had all along for the half-understood, but I inhabited those books like a native. The records were the same; songs about dreams, darkness, orphans, love, loss and solitude. The French do atmosphere like professionals. They know how to pull a pose out of a poor show. And they love a circus.

I learned the french peasant reverence for food, the pleasures of working your way in a fat land. Maybe our disrespect for food comes from our thinner land, our tougher weather up north. I learned the french idea of beauty care, with warning lights for cellulite. I knew the lures of hypochondria, philosophy and revolution. To my mind it was a well-rounded education.

Lesson Thirteen: in which Françoise and John leave town to go and live in the country, and I wonder if they hadn't put the ad in the paper themselves. Françoise left me her old postcards, some records, and a cookbook. I started going to Volta's again on a Saturday, and some of my friends have been saying lately they're glad I came out of my french phase, that they'd got tired of my enigmatic looks and half-finished sentences. Others think I actually did turn french for a while but it washed out. However my closest friend, who shall remain nameless, thinks it was a permanent change of atoms.

TREIZE

TEA WITH MARCEL PROUST

Ballymahoola, Cork, Ireland, Tuesday.

Dear Marcel Proust,

I am writing to ask if you would agree to an interview for our magazine, MADELEINE. I enclose the last issue so you can see what we're like - out on the Celtic Rim I know, but no less ardent for that. To interview you would be the ne plus ultra *of my term as editor. I suppose that writers as famous and as dead as you would rather be left alone, but put yourself in my shoes: a scoop like this would set MADELEINE on her feet.*

Looking forward to your response,

Yours,

Elspeth Rattigan

102 Boulevard Haussman, Paris, Thursday.

Dear Elspeth Rattigan,

I am in your shoes and happy to be interviewed for about an hour. Please find me at home at the above address at the time of your convenience (after 3 pm).

Yours,

Marcel Proust

Marcel Proust's salon is so discreetly full of furniture, furnishings and bric-à-brac that it's hard to know where the person leaves off and his setting begins. His white wing collar points through his brocade jacket to the mirror opposite. His dark rosy shawl moves into dark rosy islands in the flock wallpaper. Tea is served, with sandwiches in the english style. His housekeeper Céleste tends him like a shadow; she has his requests before he's finished them. Marcel Proust, fine-tuned, fine-tended, is the epitome of all the pictures I've ever seen of him; if he'd lived longer he could only have looked more intense, his eyes bigger and more bottomless, his face more politely in attendance to the rest of him and the rest of us.

ELSPETH   We called our magazine MADELEINE in honour of your great moment. Research has revealed that it's the best known fact about you, that you had a violent *déjà vu* with a cake called a *madeleine*, dunked in a teaspoon of tea, and subsequently wrote a vast work in search of lost time. Why the *madeleine*? Could it have happened with fruit cake?

MARCEL   I ate *madeleines* rarely, fruit cake never at all. It could happen to someone else with fruit cake I suppose, someone in Ireland. For me the *madeleine* and its shell shape were reassuring, banal, easily digested, like the best of my past, and infinite, like the worst.

ELSPETH   When I first read the episode of the tea and cake I wished, as many readers must, that I could have such a clear moment to set me on course. I was sure this was something which had happened to you, not something you invented.

MARCEL   The trick is not to know. Fiction tells the truth so much better than the truth can, so much more truthfully. The trick is not to know one from the other. That's how you're saved.

ELSPETH   From what?

MARCEL   Vicissitude. I like that word. It has just the right length, strength and anxiety. You find the right word and you're saved.

ELSPETH   So you did have a great moment?

MARCEL   I had quite a few, which gradually crystallised - more gradually than I would have chosen. But I was always looking for moments, and success usually favours the persistent hunter, first with quantity, then with understanding.

ELSPETH   What do you think now about the way you wrote the *madeleine* episode?

MARCEL   The dead don't read, and their memory is even more capricious than the memory of the living, but if I read it again I'm sure I would want to change it. The truth is always in transition. Yet that episode has a peculiar fixity. I don't need to read it again to feel the tight whorls unfold.

ELSPETH   Like the paper flowers in the japanese game that you put in water and they open out.

MARCEL   I still like those. The slow revelation of what you could not have guessed.

He drinks his tea with terrible care, as if taking medicine, and eats several sandwiches fast. His eyes are closer together than I'd thought from his pictures, where their largeness always held me; his cheeks are fuller, his black hair more densely on the verge of wild.

ELSPETH   The last years of your writing were done in bed, in the cork-lined room. That is the other well-known fact. It was after the death of your mother in 1905. You'd always been considered delicate, especially by your mother. Your father was all for brusqueness and not mollycoddling the boy. You could say your mother won. Was the cork-lined room in honour of her?

MARCEL   I felt close to her there. And to my grandmother. They did keep me close to them always. They were the most familiar creatures to me, even after they died, especially after I died.

ELSPETH   Is being delicate the same as being ill in french?

MARCEL   Yes. But being ill in french has always been a very sweeping gesture; it's not something idly undertaken.

ELSPETH   Life as a long written illness is not everyone's cup of - choice.

MARCEL   It wasn't mine. It was hard being locked in with unanswerable questions pounding in my head. How scrupulous did I have to be? Could I let in any new world if I hadn't fully written the old? But I didn't live it as illness, I lived it as health, I looked after it. I gave it special hours. I slept - or tried to - when others were awake; I wrote when others were asleep. I fed it what it needed and it flourished.

ELSPETH   You have asthma don't you. You were often in bed when you were young. Being so much indoors and so protected must have meant that the external world boggled the mind when you went out, so that you couldn't take too much of it.

MARCEL   My mind boggled and my knees knocked, my ankles shook. Onlookers might have said my eyes rolled. But we were polite in those days. We were very polite. I retired to the cork-lined room to write down whatever had boggled me and so to set it straight.

ELSPETH   And it ramified didn't it? In the nature of the human boggle, it grew roots with root hair till eventually it covered everything.

MARCEL   Yes. I had to keep very still and not hear anything I hadn't chosen. I wanted exactitude in the same way as I wanted pleasure - endlessly.

ELSPETH   Where do you think your talent for abstraction comes from?

MARCEL   From France. From asthma. The French take pride in abstraction; it can look supercilious to foreigners, but it brings its own passions. Words aren't abstract, they're life itself if you need them as I did. Understanding isn't abstract if it brings a good night's sleep.

ELSPETH   Vast repute isn't abstract if it brings you readers, researchers, devotees and fellow-celebrities who would read you on their desert islands. How do you feel about them?

MARCEL   What do you mean, their desert islands?

ELSPETH   It's a radio programme, you choose 8 records, a book and a luxury.

MARCEL   I like the idea of being read on a desert island. It corresponds to how it was to write it.

ELSPETH   What book would you take? Traditionally the Bible and Shakespeare are already there, though I suppose for a Frenchman they would make it Racine.

MARCEL   Ruskin? Or a completely empty, beautifully bound volume.

ELSPETH   And what luxury would you take ?

MARCEL   8 records would already be a luxury.

We begin a professional pause. Marcel pulls his shawl closer. The slight shift repositions him among the stuff of the salon, the furniture, the clocks, drapes and fol de rols. Bad for the asthma, I would have thought. How would this interview have gone if we'd held it in Ballymahoola in the back snug of a spirit store, hands-on-hot-whiskeys, amid a shuffling of boots? Ah now Marcel lad, the world as book you know, that's for the birds.

ELSPETH   The length of your work, about thirteen average books, must make the desert island ration look mean. Do you think you would have written shorter if you'd written at the end rather than the beginning of the twentieth century?

MARCEL   Yes, I would have been less rich with less leisure. But with the leisure to do it I would have done it the same. Except I would have finished it.

ELSPETH   You think you could have finished it?

MARCEL   I could have called it finished and the penance done.

ELSPETH   I think people like it unfinished, gaping like life. They like to imagine that if you'd lived for ever the book would have continued to expand, that there would have been new lost time, with a new sentence, a new phrase, a rustle through the pages as they shifted to let it in. People like to think they're infinite. That's why they become addicted to computers. You would have enjoyed the word processor; it rustles pages silently, and you can press Erase, and Find, and Justify. How presumptuous! Forgive me. I've never interviewed anyone dead before.

MARCEL   *De rien,* Madame. You're the first to have asked.

Céleste comes by in a desultory dutiful way. The dead can still take tea and the housekeeper can check the state of the pot. I scrutinize the way Marcel looks at her but can find nothing; it's as if he's looking down a corridor. He has a polite public look, like a photograph of himself: the seer seen and holding still. All the constructs, all the tight weaves and loose associations, all that serendipitous gazing at past time have made Marcel a polished performer. The more I look at him the more

I feel like the blind leading the dead. With the blind woman's surefootedness and the dead man's opaque suit.

ELSPETH   I'm curious about what you didn't write - not just what you would have written if you'd lived longer, but what you couldn't write.

MARCEL   I wrote about everything as far I knew it, knit together in the way I needed it to be.

ELSPETH   And now? As far as you know it now?

MARCEL   Now I know even less.

ELSPETH: But you did make decisions about what to write?

MARCEL   They didn't feel like decisions, they felt like seductions. The net was thrown out and I was hauled in.

He was matter-of-fact, as if years of thinking had somewhere crystallized into this. Show me the boy of twelve throwing his scarf over his shoulder and I'll show you the man in his shawl, someone said, or words to that effect. I was thinking that he hadn't written about everyone, there were slices of truly lost time - or unopened cans of worms. He hadn't written about his brother, for example. Muffled in his shawl, with a brave wing collar flying out in 1993 he still forgot. Siblings have the most oblivion in the world.

ELSPETH   Why in your book does the male narrator fall in love with women when you yourself have always loved men? Why was the prisoner Albertine and not Albert?

MARCEL   I loved the covertness of love more than love, and love more than the beloved. This was what I knew, the idea of it, the anticipation. Albert or Albertine, perhaps it makes no difference. Jealousy, desire, fruitless witless passion dependent on the inaccessibility of the beloved, all this is old as society. A prisoner is a prisoner is a prisoner.

ELSPETH   Whose prisoner were you?

MARCEL   My mother's?

ELSPETH   What did she think of your writing?

MARCEL   She liked the fact of it, I don't feel she was ever honest about what she thought of it, but she was proud and protective.

ELSPETH   And if she'd lived to read *Remembrance of Things Past*?

MARCEL   She would have felt suffocated.

ELSPETH   You mean she'd become the prisoner? Maybe you'd like to interview her and ask!

Marcel smiles and Céleste passes, glancing at him; across his upper face a flicker of irritated comfort settles for a moment.

ELSPETH   Did you ever think of writing under a woman's name? If it's the same damn thing, Albert or Albertine.

MARCEL   It would have unseated everything to use a pseudonym, a man's or a woman's name. I would have joined the characters.

ELSPETH   But you do join them don't you? You're everywhere in the book.

MARCEL   That's why the name on the cover has to be mine. Then I can't be accused of petty deception, only major deception, which is much more interesting.

ELSPETH   You published the first part of your novel yourself didn't you.

MARCEL   No one would touch it in the beginning. They thought I was a windbag with a pain. But I wanted it to be read by people outside my small circle, by people who would buy something to read for a train journey.

ELSPETH   Some train journey your readers need! Across vast continents! You'd need a private compartment and copious refreshment. Air travel has not been kind to writers like you. You were more an armchair traveller weren't you, the reality always bound to disappoint. What were your greatest pleasures as a child? As an adult?

MARCEL   As a child, my mother's kiss, walking by the river, reading in the garden. As an adult, longing for all that.

ELSPETH   Some people find that hard to believe.

MARCEL   Music also. Always the finest pleasure.

ELSPETH   Were all your pleasures fine?

MARCEL   Apart from the ones which were anguished.

ELSPETH   Do you think you would have liked to write now, in this late twentieth century climate for talking about private anguish and private pleasure?

MARCEL   No, I liked our games, our secrets, our façade. I liked our naive world; it left more to the imagination. Without deception, without adultery, there's no passion.

ELSPETH   You enjoyed breaking rules? Or you enjoyed rules?

MARCEL   It's the same thing.

ELSPETH   Do you have a good memory?

MARCEL   I remember very little. Not nearly enough to convince me.

ELSPETH   To convince you of what?

MARCEL   To convince who of what?

ELSPETH   You.

MARCEL   No, I think it was someone else. I wasn't convinced about him.

ELSPETH   Why did you accept to be interviewed?

MARCEL   Vanity. The vanity of the dead is even more insinuating than the vanity of the living. Why did you want to interview me? Why not James Joyce?

ELSPETH   Because reading you makes me sneeze.

MARCEL   What does that prove?

ELSPETH   That I understand you. James Joyce doesn't make me sneeze. He makes me feel like an ant-heap.

I have a sudden vision of Marcel Proust and other dead french writers out and about in the streets, peering at crowds in public places, across thou-shalt-not-walk-on-the grass, shoulder to shoulder with poets, painters, novelists and the occasional bemused park keeper pricking art with his litter stick.

MARCEL   Is that so? Is that so?

ELSPETH   I first heard of you in a cartoon when I was a child. A big woman is leaning against the counter of a bookshop, browsing, her petticoat showing under her coat. A spiv in a sharp hat and mac says to her: Excuse me Madam, your Proust is showing.

MARCEL   What did that make you think?

ELSPETH   That Proust was a part of the adult world which I could enjoy in secret, from the adult fiction section of the library, under P. When I read *Swann's Way* the secret part of the adult world formed into a series of words like sonorous, limpid and vacant.

MARCEL   And then you sneezed!

ELSPETH   Did you know that in sex education they try to teach children about orgasm by the example of the sneeze?

MARCEL   They don't suggest reading me!

ELSPETH   Your work hasn't so much enjoyed readership as reputation. What would it take to make a great Proust revival?

MARCEL   I don't think society revives things.

ELSPETH   It revives clothes. It tries to revive values.

MARCEL   But fails.

ELSPETH   Maybe full unemployment and the abolition of TV would do it. As it is people are too busy saving time to be interested in lost time, especially someone else's. And most people are daunted by your long sentences.

MARCEL   I didn't have it in mind to be popular.

ELSPETH   What did you have in mind?

MARCEL   To write myself down in my world while it lasted.

ELSPETH   Did you never think that indulgent?

MARCEL   No. We're all exemplary, if we take the time to look. To write myself down was to write down any person. It wasn't my privilege, it was my duty.

ELSPETH   Did you think this as you were writing?

MARCEL   Not exactly. There was nothing else that mattered as much, that was all I knew. It made me feel holy.

ELSPETH   And now, now that you haven't written for 70 years, in the wake of your epoch-making work -

MARCEL   Thank you.

ELSPETH   How does the obsession look now?

MARCEL   Still harping on my mother?

ELSPETH   You suggested it. Or was it your grandmother?

MARCEL   My grandmother translates into my aunt.

ELSPETH   And your aunt into a cup of tea.

MARCEL   I do sometimes think about *madeleines*.

ELSPETH   Recently someone dramatized your search for lost time and called the play *A Waste of Time*.

MARCEL   Probably right.

ELSPETH   But you'd do the same again?

MARCEL   It would be even longer.

He smiled, and a natty twenty one year old mingled with the wry recluse of fifty. I hope I knew when to take my leave. I hope the warmth was not imaginary as he shook my hand in the salon. Céleste showed me out. I wished I'd told him how I've always enjoyed his long sentences, climbing aboard and setting off, not knowing what. And then the sneeze.

Dear Marcel Proust,

I enclose the new issue of MADELEINE with our interview. Thank you. Already we've been asked if we're going to do any more interviews with dead writers. James Joyce has been suggested. Do you think Baudelaire would agree? Savage and bitter Baudelaire: he'd be a strong taste for hungry readers.

Thank you again for the interview. I'm glad there's life after the Great Work, whoever lives it. It was a pleasure.

Yours

Elspeth Rattigan

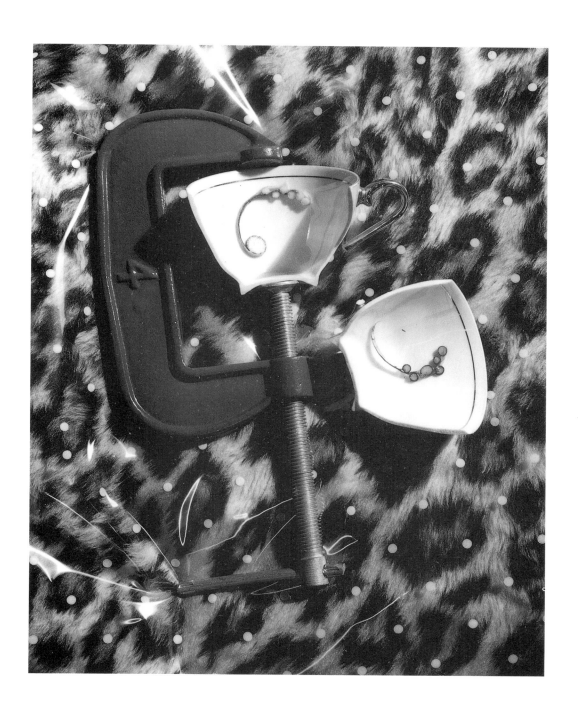

FLOWERS OF EVIL

Five free translations from Baudelaire

LXXXII

SYMPATHY FOR THE DEVIL

What thoughts drop
into your empty head
from this sky blighted
like your future life
you pagan?
Insatiable
for the dark
and the odd I find
my pride in shingly
skies, my dreams
funereal throughout
the clouds, my heart
dancing in the breaks
of light between
the breaks of darkness.

LXIX

MUSIC

Music often takes me
like a sea to
my pale star
I set sail in the mist
the air is huge
I breathe in
I puff out
I ride the backs
of waves of the night,
the good wind shivers me
the convulsed water lulls
me glassy
into despair.

XXIV

I LOVE YOU LIKE

I love you like the vault of night
O pot of silence, pot of sadness,
even more when you run away,
when you clock on the miles
that keep me from
the great blue yonder.
I step in I leap up like
a chorus of worms on a corpse
and I adore, you displeased you
cruel beast, how cold and then how
beautiful you become, my night flower.

XXXIV

THE CAT

Come walk velvet on my heart,
let me sink into your metal
precious eyes, let me see
my woman there, let me stroke
her back as you ply your head
let me tipple your body
elastic, like hers, sweet
beast, deep and cold,
cutting and slitting
like a dart through
honey, that dangerous
smell at swim in
your dark body.

XIX

THE GIANT

When lusty Nature bred monsters every day
I would have lived beside a young giant
like a pleasured cat at the queen's feet,
I would have watched her flower
all over in her terrible games,
body and soul I would have guessed
from her cloudy eyes what grew
in her hot dark heart, I would have
run at my leisure her huge form,
climbed her vast knees and sometimes
in summer under unhealthy sun, weary,
laid out on the land, slept the sleep
of the heatless in the shade of her breasts
like a village at the bottom of a mountain.

ARTHUR RIMBAUD'S NAME

(As Stéphane Mallarmé told Rémy de Gourmont)

Since you ask, suddenly Arthur Rimbaud's name came up, lulled in on our smoke one Tuesday afternoon and lay infused among us. I didn't know him but I saw him once at the Bad Boys' dinner - why they invited me I don't know. He had this bold exaggeration, this bad/good girl of the people look, like Carmen or Joan of Arc: Arthur of Elsewhere, sumptuous disorderly, meteor whizzing past shouting No past! No future! Total transformation! Now! Literature wasn't ready for him; his bed was not made and he did not sleep in it, he provoked, he sulked, he suckled the chat he caused, this exotic Someone, born and burnt out alone, an exiled angel with oval face, pale blue eyes, light brown hair, and great laundrywoman's hands red and chilblained, which wrote some fine lines, *mon cher* de Gourmont, while that sulky mouth recited none of them. Time did not pass it exploded. He roared round Europe with Verlaine, drunk on reciprocity and visions. How far do you need to go? How far East and South when you have no Future? The few syllables of ARTHUR RIMBAUD afloat on our smoke sent us into a ponder, since you ask, where silence like a drowning man fell.

THE DRUNKEN BOAT

Free translation from Rimbaud

The River said nothing
The tugs had let go
Red Indians had shot them down
I was skidding past all the cargo
In the world I was deaf
As an infant and I ran!
I tumbled like an unloosed Peninsula
Awake as a god in a storm
Lighter than a cork
I danced on the waves ten
Nights till the green water
Chopped my little Boat
Like a child who
Bites into an apple

And then I swam in the Poem
Of the Sea, suffused with stars and
Ravishingly pale, washed in blue and
Green and red and rolling in
Love I knew the sky and the walls
The whorls the rushes of light
Sometimes a thoughtful corpse drifted by
I knew the night the dawn the rise of doves
And I saw what you think you saw

I saw the sun low
I dreamed the night green
I followed the swell
I heard the sap rise
The phosphor sing
I launched at reefs
I punctured the ocean
I bumped into Florida
I saw whales ferment
And panthers' eyes
Huge snakes devoured by bed bugs
I saw the horizon crash into the void
Glaciers silver suns afloat in
Mother of pearl scorching sky
Twisted trees strong
Black flavours

I would have liked to show you
The gold and the blue
The foaming flowers that
Rocked my trip that
Winged me
Believe me
Sometimes I lulled the sea
Like a woman praying
Slapped by gull sounds and gull shit
Sometimes the drunken boat was
Lost tossed in the birdless sky

No one would have fished me out
Me the bringer of poets' best
Jam and lichen and grollies
Me the electric moonstruck boy
The wild plank the dark sea horse
Me the trembler in a Maelstrom
Me the weaver of Blue Yonders
Of continents of stars and
Islands with delirious skies

Me I wept like a baby
I missed Europe

Dawns are always dreadful
Inertia has a bitter taste when you're
Drunk with it when you're
Trapped in the traffic
Can't move can't face
The slipstream or
The bridges' terrible eyes

Burst boat burst!
I want to go to sea!
I want a cold black puddle
To launch my toy boat
And me

THE STRANGE FETE OF
LE GRAND MEAULNES

Henri Alban Fournier, pen-name Alain-Fournier, is known for one novel, Le Grand Meaulnes, *a story of adolescent quest and frustration. At the beginning of the First World War he wrote to his brother-in-law and good friend Jacques Rivière from the trenches. He was killed a few weeks later.*

Saint-Rémy wood, September 1914

Dear Jacques,

The silence is menacing at night, filled with the life stories of the dead that flash and then hang in the air. This is not just a graveyard, it's also a suspended library of the shortest stories in the world. Still, it's a comforting thought for a writer if it gets down to that in the end, the slim tale which we've practised to death hanging like everyone's favourite mist over dawn water. When I can't sleep, which is most nights, it's not my life story that flashes by, it's my novel, getting shorter all the time and moulding itself, I imagine, to changes in me that I don't yet know. If *Le Grand Meaulnes* is my message in a bottle, I'd better make my peace with it, shrink it to size. Maybe that will do instead of sleep.

You're the only person I can tell it to, especially from here, at the Front. What a joke! It's not the front it's the darkest rear end of Europe! I didn't know you in the childhood days where Meaulnes grew, which makes it easier to tell you. We could have been a different novel, you and

I, but maybe not written by me! An odd compliment I know. Take it how you will. Here's *Le Grand Meaulnes* at this week's size; by next week it might have shrunk down to a haiku.

From the first Meaulnes and I were the perfect pair. He was restless and I was a homebird, François the frightened, safe in the fold of his father's village school. As soon as Meaulnes came into our rural world of justice and good, with his head in a cloud of knowing, I knew he'd show me too. And he did. Within weeks. It was the Christmas event of going to fetch my grandparents from the station in the cart. Meaulnes wanted to go, and when someone else was chosen he went anyway, he harnessed the mare and was gone before anyone knew.

Now I can say *I* knew - and what luxury it is to know something in the middle of the night in a wood in the back end of nowhere - I knew Meaulnes would go further than any of us ever had, he'd take the mare and cart and go beyond the station, beyond the village, he'd escape and be cast up, lone and triumphant like Robinson Crusoe. It wasn't just that he was bigger than the rest of us, it was some perpetual alert he had even in the classroom, to the horizon, the edge of the envelope.

Of course the mare and cart came back on their own, no sign of Meaulnes and the mare was tired. Meaulnes showed up several days later, exhausted, hungry and enchanted. I was so curious it hurt. Here was the rocket my rustic life needed. He laid his clues like a magician: the silk waistcoat for example, with the mother-of-pearl buttons. I saw it on his bed. "Will you be off again soon?" I asked. "Will you take me?" "I can't take you," he said. "I don't know where it is, I've lost a piece of the map. I'd take you but I don't know the way." "We'll find it together," I told him, and my homebird heart surged. Meaulnes was enigmatic for weeks.

Losing maps does make you master of suspense, and the waistcoat helped, the proof, the lure, the mother-of-pearl buttons gleaming at the bottom of his bed.

One night he told me the story. The mare had got a loose nail in her shoe, and he'd fixed it but she'd kicked him, knocking him out. He had no idea where he was, he'd just bowled along in our fast winter light, till suddenly he was lost and the mare was gone. You know the story of Alice falling asleep by the river and going down the rabbit hole after the White Rabbit with the pocket watch, and thereafter nothing went according to known reality? This was like that.

The mare knocked him out and he continued to be knocked out even after he came round. He froze in sheepfolds, he shivered in his smock, he was lost for a day and a night; he was hungry, he remembered his favourite vision: in a long green room, with hangings like leaves in light so gentle you could taste it, by the window a woman sat sewing, her back to him, waiting for him to wake up.

Onward: you know, towards the unreachable. How you shiver with pleasure and dread! By series of delay and distraction Meaulnes arrives at a long avenue. I've loved those as long as I can remember, the way they draw you down with their parallel lines of trees, like a horizontal church spire, and then the curve that hides the house in which more secrets are hidden, revelations delayed. This avenue is like that, lined with coaches, carts and carriages. The first words Meaulnes overhears are from children: "Tonight at the fête we can do what we want. Children make the rules here."

At the end of the avenue the *château* dips into the lake. The air is glacial and calm. In this brinkish place between childhood and love you can spend as long as you like. Costumes are laid out on beds. You can become someone else. You explore the *château* and come upon the long green room of your vision where a woman is playing the piano, her back to you.

You know how you join in the fête you come upon by chance. How you wear the silk waistcoat you find on the bed, meet mysterious Frantz and immediately he entrusts you with a secret which you'll keep for ever? Soon you realise it is not your mother playing the piano, it is Frantz's sister Yvonne. As you listen to her play you feel the calmest happiness in the world, for a moment.

These nights when I sleep it's because I still have that moment in my head. Am I mad or just nostalgic? For my childhood or for my novel? For François, Meaulnes or Yvonne?

The next day Meaulnes meets Yvonne down by the lake and in the soft winter sun he tells her she's beautiful, just like that. He's transfixed and she's saying: "What's the use? What's the use?" Then she's gone. This was how he told it or I wrote it or what you will - I'm counting on you! Will something for me!

Mes souliers sont rouges

Adieu mon amour

Mes souliers sont rouges

Adieu sans retour

Meaulnes' story rocked about between unasked questions. I couldn't resist the rush of eternity; homebirds never can. I'd follow it to the ends of my earth. He knew that. Maybe that was why he needed me, to have someone listen, as my father told my mother about his fishing trips and she listened as if he'd ridden the world and laid the spoils at her feet? Or did he need me to get involved? Did he need me to help find Yvonne because he knew he'd disappear? Did he need me to take over?

We did piece the map together, we found Yvonne and the lost *domaine*. We brought it all into reality, or perhaps it was simply ourselves and our growing up and reality was still far away? I was about 17. Meaulnes was 19. He married Yvonne, she died giving birth to their daughter and then Meaulnes was gone. I was left. This was what I was for after all: François Keeps House. I tried to spell it out in the novel but I fell into such twists trying to resolve things to the satisfaction of everyone - I was a pleaser you see, an irresolute - that I had to dispense with Meaulnes.

Aha, you're thinking, the homebird is actually a bird of prey. Maybe I drove Meaulnes off into the sunset with his daughter on his back; maybe I am the greedy horizon boy, not him. If I hadn't intervened maybe Yvonne would not have died. Maybe the homebird was a messer. The order in which things happened veers about in my head every night. There's no orthodox version any more. Maybe this is the liberation of telling and re-telling your only tale. You no longer know what happened. You can't remember an untainted version. There never was one. The story you die with is not the true one it's just the last.

The current story is that I invented Meaulnes. I didn't invent Yvonne but I moved her from Paris where I met her, mooncalf that I was, to the *château* in the *domaine*, in fact to an amalgam of *châteaux* and *domaines*, manor houses with avenues and lakes, places I knew when I was growing up. I wanted a story worthy of the best of my childhood. What I wrote turned out just as worthy of the worst. It's hard to like yourself when you spread yourself into several characters and several hundred pages.

Le Grand Meaulnes was named after a village near where I grew up. I was, most of the time, François the narrator, the homebird. There's always been a narrator in me, an anxious keeper of the keys, a curator, a housewife who keeps tabs. Meaulnes was the adventurer who fished the future in seven league boots and said little. There was such power in appearing and disappearing without saying why. The days I was Meaulnes were the days I went black and blind into the future. Maybe it wasn't power. Maybe it was terror. While François kept by and comforted all the people Meaulnes had upset.

I was obsessed with Meaulnes and François; even now sometimes I wake up and decide: today I'm François, today I'm Meaulnes, occasionally a bystander called Henri. I was obsessed with purity, which was always lost purity, there being in my aged young head(s) none to be found, or none to stay. Glimpses were the acme by the time I was 17. I couldn't hope for more than that. Which was why Yvonne had to be so hard to find and then die - women have a hard time in childbirth and fiction - thus to remain pure. And the marriage between Yvonne and Meaulnes could not work because it had not happened, because I hadn't been Meaulnes enough of the time. Do you follow?

Never explain, never complain. We write the fiction of our childhood so that the fiction of our adulthood does not overwhelm. If we're lucky we may not even see it as it finally closes in. We may be by the lake at the lost *domaine* on a calm and silent winter day, someone may be playing the piano, the fête may have begun. We may be striding away on the course of events, our daughter on our back, or our novel, into the black and blind. We do that every day here.

Yours ever,
Henri

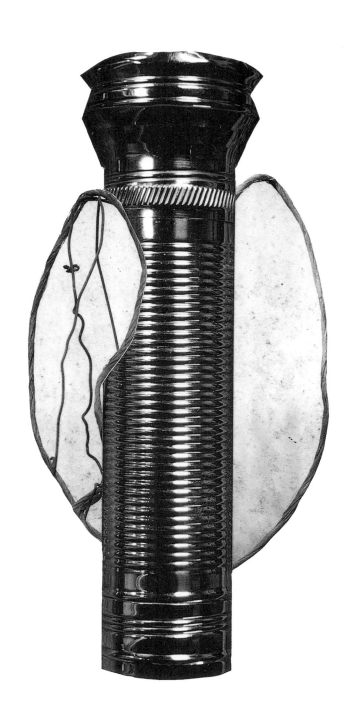

DANCING WITH MALLARME

Ian sitting on the strawbale is the image of the poet Stéphane Mallarmé. The polished Doc boots are wrong but the old black suit and white cuffs are entirely 19th century french poet even if he's never read one. Legs crossed, hands clasped around knees, eyes intent on the dancing, he's Mallarmé's costume brother. The faces are different, but the attention is the same: Ian engrossed in the dancing at the party, Mallarmé dead these one hundred years, laid out in his Complete Works in the serene *Pléiade* edition, white on black like the stars. This smooth life on India paper was not what Numa Mallarmé, the poet's father, had thought for his son; nor Elisabeth-Félicie, the poet's mother, who died when Stéphane was five: this smooth death. They were civil servants, they did not think of poetry nor talk of death. A second son Ian, born a hundred years later, had not been in their plans either.

Ian lives in a Rudolf Steiner village, an old estate with walled gardens and lawns, huge trees with fat rope swings that fly you across overgrown rhododendrons and land you in soft leaf mould. The weak have inherited the earth and now they tend it. Daily traffic and daily tasks make the ex-mine-owner's mansion into a village; the solitary wounded become villagers, and the private becomes communal. Ian works each day in the walled garden; he weeds a tidy row of leeks; he caps the compost clamp with straw, he pushes a tidy barrow. Ian's mother and father, who may have lived in Croydon or Pinner, amid property or stringency, from their moment of passion did not see Ian in this village, motionless in front of the dancing, they did not see him as the image of the poet Mallarmé.

I LOOKED FOR INFINITY

I FOUND AN ABYSS

O MY MYSTERIOUS

AND BLOODY LOVE

SIT DOWN

AND DOWN YOU SIT

BESIDE ME

HOW TINY

YOU ARE

HOW COLD

Ian sits like a shy boy of seventeen though he's nearer forty seven. He might join in the dancing if he watches the moves; when he's ready. All the other villagers are on the edge of their strawbales; total attention to one thing rapidly changes into total attention to another. The children of the co-workers are into their last bursts of energy for the day: dancing whirls them silly before bed. In the games they were fiercely competitive - fierce for a Rudolf Steiner village, fierce for a nineteenth century french poet: floppy-duck racing round a chalk track on the floor, climbing frogs on strings up to the roof, musical laps, and unofficial games like strawbale jumping and falling on purpose and pushing, kicking, screaming.

"Take your partners please, it's the Rufty Tufty!" From around the room there's a rush of villagers; co-workers get up too, and their older children who look downwards and sideways to join hands. Younger children look upward, flushed as pomegranates. Straw from the bales starts to fly. Dancing and undancing children are in and out of the ragged sets.

Nearby children come to a complete halt when Ian falls off his strawbale. He falls as they do not fall in the movies, as if seized and then dropped, like a mouse from a terrified cat. He launches and rolls sideways onto the floor and lies there, collapsed at all angles of limbs and straw. There has been no struggle. It's more like a painting than a disaster movie. One of the co-workers rolls Ian onto his side and keeps the children back. The children watch in silence, respect, fascination and fear; they remember nothing but a print is taken. The polished black Docs, smudged with dust, show up under the ruckled black trousers: to see that much of them is painful, like listening to Mallarmé screaming underneath his poems.

YOUR GRAVE IS DUG

MOTHER

I'M HAUNTED

SISTER

ALL FLIGHTS ARE

FROZEN ALL WINGS

A-QUIVER

LOVE

BLUE WITH

COLD

The children soon lose interest in Ian, they're back in the fray, charging steam holes down the promenade and shrieking with laughter. Ian lies on the floor through three dances. No one touches him but two of the co-workers are keeping an eye on him. When he starts to move new children are watching with dispassionate mouth and rivetted eyes.

One or two pieces of straw fall off him, one or two more as he picks himself up. The dust ruckles are still standing on his suit as he turns towards the strawbale, then climbs onto it and reaches into the shelves behind, his jacket hoicked to take his outstretched arms, the polished Docs fully revealed with their supple creases round the ankles. He leans into the space behind the strawbales, a skewed, slight figure, hair awry like a child in a romper suit, his clothes holding him as if something always does.

Other children pass by, determined not to see what they've seen many times before: a villager scrabbling for the back of beyond. One co-worker says to the other: "Last time he took a whole grandfather clock to pieces. Good thing the shelves are backed up like that for the party. He'd have everything out." "Wonder what he's looking for." They stand a few feet back in their habitual, daily concern. "He doesn't know, that's for sure."

Ian is trying to pull out boxes but nothing will budge more than an inch. From a heap of bales in the corner of the room a child falls and starts wailing. Ian is leaning so far over the stack of bales into the shelves that he's almost off his feet, ferreting for the nearest dark thing. He did know, that was for sure, he knew better than anything, this push and pull further than he'd ever been before, every time, this grasping, dismantling velvet eye in there and his hands nearly on it.

I'M A CHILD

WITH A PALE

SMOOTH AND

BLOODY WING

I'M HELPLESS

I'M STARVING

TAKE ME IN

AND FEED

FEED ME

TO THE BRIM

Ian withdraws from the shelves, turns back slowly towards the room, one trouser leg still caught on top of a half-polished, half-scuffed boot. He sits down again on the strawbale, jacket skewed, hair awry. There's the party, there's the dancing, here are exhausted children wrapped in climbing frog strings. A half-shake, and his jacket settles. Here I am. Ian is thinner by far than Mallarmé. He has said nothing all evening.

"Take your partners please. It's Sellinger's Round!"

Music from the three piece band, a recorder player, a violinist and a guitarist, begins and a ragged circle forms, hands fumble for hands, children nip and push. Ian gets up and lets himself into the circle between a villager and a flushed child. He has their hands as they move off to the right or maybe left, then he's lost one, then the other, now they're moving again in a circle the shape of the floppy duck track, and back the other way. At every pause in the dance Ian looks at the other dancers to make sure he's doing it right; he's ready for the music to change, the step to change, he's off before it has begun, he's the keenest child at the party.

"Two lines now! Make an arch! First couple, gallop! Second couple! Third couple!"

Ian and the flushed child gallop through.

"Swing your partners now!"

Ian and the flushed child grab each other and whizz round like the clappers. For moments they might have lift-off. Then they have collision. Ian's hands loosen on the swing and the child skids across the floor, bumping breathless to a halt against a strawbale.

VERTIGO!

SPACE SHIVERS

A BIG KISS

FOR NO ONE

AT ALL

A GIDDY SOUL

WHIRLS IN THE AIR

& YOU LAND

WITH A BUMP

BESIDE HIM

LA VIE EN ROSE

La vie en rose   Life in the pink &
La rose en vie   The pink in bloom
Le mot en peut-   Could be the
Etre   Word
    rougit   blusher

LOOKING

Looking at larger and larger structures quietly

trust me   they don't come much quieter than this.

A QUESTION OF

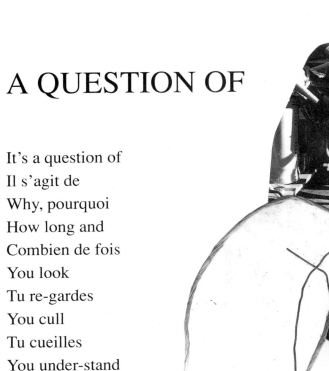

It's a question of
Il s'agit de
Why, pourquoi
How long and
Combien de fois
You look
Tu re-gardes
You cull
Tu cueilles
You under-stand
Tu comprends

A question of
Focus
Intensity
Light
& nuit,
dark.

MOTIONLESS   LA CHOSE IMMOBILE

You know empty	Tu connais le vide
You know full	Tu connais le plein
You know half	Tu connais le mi-
You know time	Tu connais le temps
You know	Tu connais
You know	Tu connais
You know	Tu connais
it purifies	ça purifie
the blood	le sang

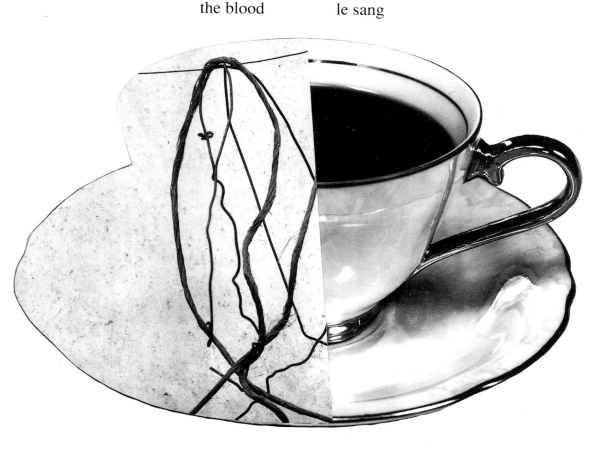

MORGAN. 93

WILD LETTERS

Hélas ma fille, que mes lettres sont sauvages.
Alas my daughter, my letters are wild.
                              Madame de Sévigné, 1671.

What was a wild letter in France, where letters were an art form, in 1671 when readers were high flyers ? A creature of chance, rare as a wild garden in a civilisation whose gardens looked like a game of chess, whose social rituals were glacial. Madame de Sévigné writes as she thinks as she looks out on the world and in on her feelings; she feels a chat coming on and she writes it as it comes, Alas and Thank God. She comments on what she does; she's an aristocrat, she's used to considering her position; but she also slips the noose and runs on like a lonely woman in a large *château*.

I've been pacing about all day, doing this and that, walking in the garden, not knowing what, till just now I realised I wanted to sit down at my desk and write to you.

To her a good letter like an average day has tired moments, interruptions and bursts of enthusiasm. She can turn a fine sentence like a well-educated woman, and has her correct names and her good ear, her well-loved idioms and the latest phrase from Pascal or Racine all in perfect working order; but she'll go anywhere, she'll follow her drift, fall into her plunges, her pauses, pace her affections, admit her prejudice and the limits of her language:

Hélas! que vais-je vous dire du milieu de mes bois?

From the middle of her woods in Brittany she says the silence of the trees and the absence of her daughter in the space of an echoey alexandrine: the invincible alexandrine, eater of feeling. *Hélas!* she says again, and the silvery introduction it makes on the ear turns round her apology; she's only playing at having a problem. What shall I tell you? she wonders out loud. Why aren't you here? she asks within.

My letters to you are food and drink to me, she tells her daughter, who moved after her marriage to Provence, several weeks travel in those days from Brittany. Madame was distraught at the separation; she wept and she wrote exhaustive love letters to her lost one. The daughter's letters aren't preserved, but we don't sense white heat being fanned at the other end. Daughters of the 20th century might find this mother's love too rich a mixture for comfort. She wrote so often and so long ago that we phoners and faxers and airplaning lovers read her letters as fiction. Not that we doubt this mother's love; on the contrary we believe her too well, as we believe and relish fictional mothers all over the literary world. She protests too much, she yearns like a lover, she counts the days and imagines the trace of steps that each must take and how they do not intertwine from Brittany to Provence. She creates herself on her pages and we believe her as we believe Madame Bovary rather than Flaubert. She doesn't create her daughter in her letters, she's already done that in her belly. She creates herself so that she in her turn can lie in her letters, a mother at the heart of her daughter's household, tied up with ribbon in a writing desk drawer.

See how naked is the letter-writer 300 years on. The barest facts are enough. We know Madame de Sévigné was a widow at 25 and an orphan at 7. Twice abandoned was she twice toughened? Was she doubly in need of her daughter because doubly daughter herself? She had saints and warriors in her ancestry; she was an aristocrat in a century that brought social standing to a pursuit in its own right; she had two households, one in Paris and one in Brittany; she frequented the Royal Court of Louis the 14th and wrote about it in her letters like the piece of domestic theatre it was, with its press of periwigs and hangers-on. Widows were focal at court. Madame lost her husband as many did then, in a duel. Guesses vary as to whether she remained true to his memory or vowed not to get burned again; either way she brought up her two children alone (with her servants) and remained alone (with her servants) for the rest of her life. She was trained for society and adept at solitude, a laughing Trappist at her writing desk and a woman-about-Paris in her coach and four.

Orphans are wailers of the wilderness. If you were a 17th century aristocrat you could wail in the wilderness of the page. Madame de Sévigné slid into literacy like a babe into arms. The pleasure of having a voice! If you have a voice then use it: talk on and talk away, do not heed where you go and whence you come, just keep close to your life and you'll keep close to your daughter, close to yourself and the state of your blood.

The best letters are written by those who would rather talk and touch, who write in a rush of desire. You learn about everyday life, butter in Provence or how the new row of trees is coming on, how to haggle your taxes, how they're doing their hair these days at Court. These things are crucial to Madame's days and therefore to her passion for her daughter.

Madame travelled to see her daughter in Provence as well as more local visits to other correspondents, and she wrote en route. En Route was a broad and dangerous place in those days.

We were in the boat by six on the finest day in the world. I had the coach placed so that the sun didn't come in. We lowered the windows and out the front we had a splendid view, while the little peepholes at the side gave us a look in every other direction. We had hot soup in the coach; things are getting very refined on the Loire these days.

We *blasé* travellers of the late twentieth century regard as mythical a journey slow enough to include letters; we're even beyond sending postcards of airplanes from airports. In our lazy minimalism we shuffle off the names of cities along the way and score on stories of delays. Madame told her journeys as she told her days and her cures: to one from whom she would keep nothing.

To be educated in the 17th century was to be initiated into elegance. The *crème de la crème* of Tzarist Russia enjoyed pretending to be french; it gave the edge to your claustrophobia. In South and North America brothels were finest french by the mid-19th century. Elegance and lustiness, the high hand and the common touch, Madame de Sévigné inherited.

Whatever our new misgivings in the 20th century as daughters with language, we wouldn't want to lose Madame and her letters. They are part of the long line of private howls that get louder the nearer we get to the present time.

But my God where <u>haven't</u> I seen you here? Why do these thoughts keep banging through my head? There's no place, no spot, in the house, in the church, in the countryside, in the garden, where I haven't seen you once and where I still don't see you.

Literature would not want to lose her either. The leather-bound selection of the letters became quintessential private library after it was published in the 18th century, gilded, marbled and leather-bound; the several volumes of *Pléiade* edition impress with their thousands of pages of intimacy, tender and angry and silly and apologetic, always close to the bone. For more than a 100 years in France Madame was the model of a mother writing to her daughter, a genial giver of rules. *Look where I am,* she says at the beginning of a letter, and we look. We may not have heard of the place, but we look at her looking, we spread with her into her new spot on earth. Or on water:

Here's a strange one for you! I'm in a boat, going with the flow, far from my château and, I think I can safely say, crazy!

Before Christmas 1689 she writes about the fine cold days.

I heard in Paris how winter days weren't as short as they used to be. We really notice it up here in Brittany where there's nothing to distract us. At five every day my son is still reading, the day doesn't end till 5.30. And there, my dear daughter, you have a proper spiel to fill a letter going nowhere!

We like to regularize our history: Madame de Sévigné suffered great losses, but she was fortunate: she was rich and educated, a lady of leisure, she wrote letters at a time when literacy was a social grace second to none, when women were arbiters of taste, mistresses of *salons*, and when letters, which women were thought to write best, were among the top three media with theatre, written in verse by men, and fiction, often written by men pretending to be women. *These women have a way with words*, pondered Bossuet, orator, agoniser of faith, henchman of literature and Madame de Sévigné's contemporary. *They make the words fit the feeling. They seem to know how.* He sounds incredulous. The connection between words and feeling was mysterious to him: feeling is slippery, whole words get swallowed and disappear; there are vast spaces which will not come under control.

In 1215 A.D. the University of Paris directed its scholars to produce a comprehensive theory of the world. In the middle of the 17th century Bossuet and his fellow moralists were still trying. They mainly established, in language as neat and balanced as ranks of angels, that there was much to doubt. Of that doubt came a building block of western culture: theory as weapon, knowledge as power, power as elegance, with God On Our Side. Culture as everyday life, as irritation of the blood or silence in the woods, doesn't win the respect of generations to come. They want to know what was decided, what happened on the largest scale, which countries changed hands and what were the new discoveries in the known world. They want to be hit by the absolute and incontrovertible and then they want to be able to hit back.

What was the comprehensive theory of the world? What were the limits of the world in 1215? In 1671? Perhaps they were the same as they are now, give or take a galaxy, a tectonic plate, a camcorder or a cup of tea. From a dog-end of a village in the pouring rain Madame de Sévigné writes that she'll write when her feet have warmed up. On a better day she breathes the country air and declares you could grow plump on its warm dampness. What do we think of Madame de Sévigné's feet? They're familiar. It's reassuring to learn of cold feet in 1671 in rural France; cold feet 300 years on are just as cold, warm dampness just as plump.

For the tidy mind Madame's wild letters are themselves a theory of the world, a *cogito sensible,* as Foucault said. Warm, spontaneous, divergent, intuitive, graceful, funny, they follow her feelings first and then her literacy. She had a passionate reason to write, to get her days down on the page and send the page off, to talk, talk away. It won't raise the dead but it cheers the living. *Bonjour. Bonne oeuvre.* Good day. Good work.

She wrote as she would have talked, except, as the days were compressed into black and white - was her ink blue? or violet? - willy nilly you have structure and choice and you begin to ride on this, especially if you're french, you start to take your pace from the page, to show your warmth and get close to your daughter without taking another step. Flann O'Brien knew about that: his advice was always to stay at home and send postcards.

Letters were the great saviour of the 17th century leisured classes. The novels they read were often in the form of letters; letters trip the plots of plays; letters to lovers, from the deserted to the far away. Letters of yearning bore strong fruit by the 19th century in Romantic poets - men - whose poems are like letters with no readers, and no replies. The poem has to eat its own tail; the hungry poet is also the reader. Madame de Sévigné wrote letters in a culture which understood that its language had reached some kind of apôgée: anything she wanted to say she could, any silence that she wanted to conjure was hers too.

Well well dear girl I'll tell you in those woods I do honour to the moon I love so well as my dear you know. La Plessis has gone, the good padre fears the chill of dusk - me, I've never felt it; I'm with Beaulieu and my valets till eight. Really these alleys are so beautiful, so peaceful, so calm, with a silence I could never exhaust. When I think of you I think tenderly, for if I know such things it's through imagining them for you.

Maybe women writers would have wanted a comprehensive theory of the world if their written voice had developed alongside men's, but it didn't. Truth in the last few decades has shifted from the language of men to the language of women and back again several times. After a brief burst of optimism in which it seemed as if reaching the stars and walking on them - chiefly a male sport - were the first and last truth about the world, even more insistent than God, the world has become harder and harder to define, or its definitions more meaningless to more people, like utilitarianism gone mad. A comprehensive theory of the world in 1993 would just be the name of the business; like One Hour Cleaners, or Express Post or the Car That Thinks; whereas chat never dies, it cannot be contradicted or refuted, it cannot fail.

It's a source of much wailing to many women that they must borrow their history and their language from men. Madame de Sévigné borrowed with pleasure; she had her language too, one that Bossuet didn't have and Racine only in epiphanies, in verse so elevated it startles like a neat new pair of tears.

200 years later Proust grew up on Madame de Sévigné's wild letters. When we read him we read her saga of upper class life in the 17th century, her domestic understanding transformed into the end of upper class life at the beginning of the 20th century with its different dramas, different licence, different literacy. Atoms of Sévigné mingle with atoms of Proust; his time past is also hers.

Generations of readers, browsers, and instant culture fiends have drunk from Proust's cup of tea, the walking wounded and the sitting wondering, from Virginia Woolf to Marguerite Duras. New generations have drunk from theirs. Jorge Luis Borges liked this flow of books, their mingling, the underground streams, the grand waterfalls and the greedy drinking of centuries of readers. He dreamed about the book which would clarify an infinite library and was happy that as he could not find it he would have to carry on reading.

PICTURE DETAILS

COLOUR PICTURES

Frontispiece   BONJOUR: found images, postcard, laser prints, paint, wax on Arches paper.

Page 14   HARLEQUIN CUP: cellophane, G clamp, Chinese flowers, broken cup, on fabric.

Page 28   NATURE MORTE: fabric, magic wands, chaise longue, marbles, paper, broken cup, string, cellophane, glass jar, target, magazine, lead soldier, table, on carpet and copper sheet.

Page 34   DON'T KICK JUST LICK: lemon juice, salt, cellophane, magic wand, black net, chalk, coat hanger, G clamp, string, wax, on copper sheet.

Page 36   OUI I: paint, photographs, gold dust, pencil, on Langton paper.

Page 38   OUI II: paint, photographs, pencil, on Langton paper.

Page 40   OUI III: paint, photographs, pencil, on Langton paper.

Page 51   A WORD UNSAID: coathanger, string, wax, straw, lemon juice on copper sheet.

Page 64   DEJA VU: found images, paint, photographs, laser prints, pencil, on Arches paper.

BLACK AND WHITE PICTURES

The black and white pictures exist as photographs and photo-collages.

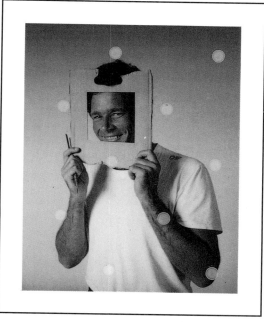

JUDY KRAVIS has published poetry, fiction, features and a study of Mallarmé. She has given readings in Ireland, France, USA and Holland, some with film and music. Her opera libretto, *Hot Food With Strangers* was performed in Ireland and London in 1991 and 1993. She teaches french literature at University College Cork.

PETER MORGAN is an artist, photographer and illustrator. He has taught at Limerick School of Art and Design since 1987. His work has been exhibited, published and collected in Ireland, Britain, USA and Italy. Collectors include BP, Holmes Marchant Productions, Mixed Media, University College Cork and The Arts Council of Ireland.

JUDY KRAVIS and PETER MORGAN have collaborated on books and films:

Packed Lunch (1988), Super 8 film
Hey! Hey! Remember me? (1988), edition of one
If One Green Bottle... (1989) Super 8 film
Rough Diamante (Road Books 1992) edition of 500
The Seventh Forum On Spare Parts (1993) edition of one